LEONARD J. ARRINGTON
MORMON HISTORY LECTURE SERIES
No. 25

What the Railroad Will Bring Us
The Legacy of the Transcontinental Railroad Corporations

by Richard Wh

T0168115

Sponsored by

Special Collections & Archives
Merrill-Cazier Library
Utah State University
Logan, Utah

Published by Merrill-Cazier Library
Distributed by Utah State University Press
Logan, UT 84322

FOREWORD

F. Ross Peterson

The establishment of a lecture series honoring a library's special collections and a donor to that collection is unique. Utah State University's Merrill-Cazier Library houses the personal and historical collection of Leonard J. Arrington, a renowned scholar of the American West. As part of Arrington's gift to the university, he requested that the university's historical collection become the focus for an annual lecture on an aspect of Mormon history. Utah State agreed to the request and in 1995 inaugurated the annual Leonard J. Arrington Mormon History Lecture.

Utah State University's Special Collections and Archives is ideally suited as the host for the lecture series. The state's land grant university began collecting records very early, and in the 1960s became a major depository for Utah and Mormon records. Leonard and his wife Grace joined the USU faculty and family in 1946, and the Arringtons and their colleagues worked to collect original diaries, journals, letters, and photographs.

Although trained as an economist at the University of North Carolina, Arrington became a Mormon historian of international repute. Working with numerous colleagues, the Twin Falls, Idaho, native produced the classic *Great Basin Kingdom: An Economic History of the Latter-day Saints* in 1958. Utilizing available collections at USU, Arrington embarked on a prolific publishing and editing career. He and his close ally, Dr. S. George Ellsworth, helped organize the Western History Association, and they created the *Western Historical Quarterly* as the scholarly voice of the WHA.

While serving with Ellsworth as editor of the new journal, Arrington also helped both the Mormon History Association and the independent journal *Dialogue*.

One of Arrington's great talents was to encourage and inspire other scholars or writers. While he worked on biographies or institutional histories, he employed many young scholars as researchers. He fostered many careers as well as arranged for the publication of numerous books and articles.

In 1972, Arrington accepted appointments as the official historian of the Church of Jesus Christ of Latter-day Saints and the Lemuel Redd Chair of Western History at Brigham Young University. More and more Arrington focused on Mormon, rather than economic, historical topics. His own career flourished with the publication of *The Mormon Experience*, co-authored with Davis Bitton, and *American Moses: A Biography of Brigham Young*. He and his staff produced many research papers and position papers for the LDS Church as well. Nevertheless, tension developed over the historical process, and Arrington chose to move full time to BYU with his entire staff. The Joseph Fielding Smith Institute of History was established, and Leonard continued to mentor new scholars as well as publish biographies. He also produced a very significant two-volume study, *The History of Idaho*.

After Grace Arrington passed away, Leonard married Harriet Horne of Salt Lake City. They made the decision to deposit the vast Arrington collection of research documents, letters, files, books, and journals at Utah State University. The Leonard J. Arrington Historical Archives is part of the university's Special Collections. The Arrington Lecture Committee works with Special Collections to sponsor the annual lecture.

'WHAT THE RAILROAD WILL BRING US'

I have taken my title from an article that Henry George wrote for the *Overland Monthly* in 1868 before the completion of the Pacific Railroad, as the combination of the Union Pacific/Central Pacific was called. George was one of the few skeptics about the benefits of the transcontinental railroad. He was afraid that the railroad would destroy his California.

Henry George, who was both a radical and a racist, thought about California in terms of white people. He loved California, praising the state's "cosmopolitanism, a certain freedom and breadth of common thought and feeling, natural to a community made up from so many difference sources, to which every man and woman had been transplanted—all travelers to some extent, and with native angularities of prejudice and habit more or less worn off."[1]

He celebrated what became the classic romantic view of the West. He claimed for California "a feeling of personal independence and equality, a general hopefulness and self-reliance and a certain large-heartedness and open-handedness which were born of the comparative evenness with which property was distributed, the high standard of wages and comfort, and the latent feeling of every one that he might 'make a strike,' and certainly could not be kept down long."[2]

He was afraid that the railroad would destroy this. The benefits of the railroad would be more than off-set by the losses Californians would incur. Speculators and "captains of industry," who employed men in "gangs," would undercut the "personal independence—the basis of all

1

virtues"—that had characterized the state and its people. George feared that the benefits of the railroads would flow to capitalists; the losses would be borne by working people. The spawn of California's millionaires would be its numerous and desperate poor.[3]

I cite George because I am sometimes accused of unfairly condemning the men who organized and ran the Central Pacific and then the Southern Pacific railroads by applying twenty-first-century standards to nineteenth-century railroad corporations and conditions. But this is not true. I am very old fashioned: I apply nineteenth-century standards.

I am far gentler than George or, on the other political extreme, Charles Francis Adams, president of the Union Pacific, who worked intimately with the big railroad men of the era—including the Associates as they called themselves or the Big Four as we remember them today. He wrote that "I have known and known tolerably well, a good many 'successful' men—'big' financially—men famous during the last half-century; and a less interesting crowd I do not care to encounter. Not one that I have ever known would I care to meet again, either in this world or the next; nor is one of them associated in my mind with the idea of humor, thought, or refinement. A set of mere money-getters and traders, they were essentially unattractive and uninteresting."[4]

Adams was hardly alone. At the end of the century, Ambrose Bierce pilloried Collis P. Huntington, the most able of the Associates, writing that "Of our modern Forty Thieves, Mr. Huntington is the surviving 36." A.A. Cohen, sometimes partner sometimes enemy, memorialized another of the Associates, Charles Crocker, in one of the classics of nineteenth century invective as "a living, breathing, waddling monument of the triumph of vulgarity, viciousness, and dishonesty."[5]

Leland Stanford, today the best remembered of the Associates inspired a litany of dismay, exasperation, and disdain from his own Associates. Huntington once wrote to Stanford that "I wish you would tell me whom to correspond with in Cal. when I want anything done; for I have become thoroughly convinced that there is no use in writing to you."[6] It "was not," Huntington noted wearily, "safe to do business with him or in other words trust him to do anything."[7]

Mark Hopkins thought Stanford's key quality was his ability to compound stupidity with laziness. "He could do it," Hopkins told Huntington of some necessary task, "but not without more mental effort than is agreeable to him."[8]

These assessments don't come from the enemies of the men who ran the railroads. They come from each other and those who worked with them. We are the ones who tend to romanticize the transcontinentals, not the people who ran them and used them.

So why were so many Americans so hostile to railroad corporations? To understand this we need to separate the railroads from the railroad corporations that controlled them. Americans loved railroads; they hated railroad corporations. To answer the question, I want to look at transcontinentals as a whole, not just the Union Pacific and Central Pacific that together constituted the first transcontinental, and I want to examine them over a broad span of a generation, 1865–1896.

My intent is to examine why they were built, whether they were built prematurely, and the consequences of building them. What I am going to say challenges one of the iconic stories of American development, which is contained in John Gast's famous 1872 lithograph, "American Progress," which made American advance inevitable and railroads the logical consequence of the advance of American pioneers.[9]

In "American Progress," Indians and bison retreated while white Americans advanced. Their vanguard came on horseback and in covered wagons. In the middle ground, farmers plowed the earth, and behind them came railroad trains and the telegraph. Floating above them all was a female figure draped in white with the star of empire on her brow, telegraph wire in one hand and schoolbook in the other.

Such a description of the American advance was already outdated when Gast printed it in 1873. It captured antebellum ideas of American progress, not the new Republican progress that came out of the Civil War. What was missing? There is no state—no federal government—in the picture. There is no Morrill Act, Homestead Act, and Railroad Land Grants. In the actual history, railroads no longer followed, they led, and because they led, most railroads were built too soon and their costs exceeded their benefits.

Things turned out pretty much how politicians and railroad men who opposed the subsidies to the transcontinentals thought they would. We got railroads we didn't need in places we didn't need them, and we promoted growth that did more harm than good. The result was dumb growth, and its ultimate cost was the emptying out of much of the interior of western North America.

The idea to build a transcontinental was old (as old goes in the United States), but for years it didn't happen because there was no private company that could afford to build it alone, and the sectional quarrel between the North and South over its route had blocked federal aid. With secession of South, the sectional obstacle disappeared, but financial obstacles remained. The government now had a rationale—the need to preserve the nation and capture Asian trade—but still did not have money to build it.

The rationale is accurately recorded on the golden spike to commemorate its completion at Promontory Summit in 1869. "May God continue the unity of our country as this Railroad unites the two great oceans of the world." The opening phrase—"May God continue the unity of our country"—referred to the Civil War, but in 1869 the Civil War had been over for four years. We didn't need a railroad to preserve the Union. It was preserved. Real building of the railroad had not even begun until the war was nearly over.[10]

The second half of the inscription—"as this Railroad unites the two great oceans of the world" referred to the trade of Asia, which the railroad was supposed to secure. Capturing the trade of Asia was an old dream, but the railroad did not capture it. Plans to build a Suez Canal were hardly secret in the 1860s. The canal was completed a few months after the transcontinental. It turned out that short canals trumped long railroads and that moving goods long distances by water was far more efficient than moving them long distances overland. True then, true now. The trade of Asia moved through the Suez.

The failure of old rationales did not lead to abandonment of plans for the transcontinental railroads but instead to new rationales. As often happens in American history, the new rationales came at the expense of the Indians. Government officials and railroad promoters quickly replaced defeating the Confederacy with defeating the Indians as a rationale for the railroad. In 1867, two years before the Pacific Railroad was completed, General William Tecumseh Sherman called the road "the solution of the Indian question."[11] This became a refrain picked up by the railroads. To quote Grenville Dodge, "Experience proves the Railroad line through Indian Territory a Fortress as well as a highway."[12] Or as Charles Francis Adams, later president of the Union Pacific, put it, "the Pacific railroads have settled the Indian question."[13] Railroads did help defeat the Indians. It took 2 ½ centuries for English Speaking people to get ½ way across the continent. Occupying the rest took only a generation. This might seem a success, but looked at more closely this was the kind of success the country could have done without. The Indian wars that the railroads helped win were often only necessary because we were building railroads whose other goal was to attract settlers and induce development. In hindsight the Plains Indian wars were tawdry little wars against desperate peoples defending their homelands. The major ones—the Red River Wars and the Sioux Wars —would not have had to be fought if not for the railroads.

The same officers who fought these wars admitted as much. Sherman recognized that "The poor Indians are starving. We kill them if they attempt to hunt and if they keep within the Reservation, they starve." Phil Sheridan admitted that "We took away their country and their means of support, broke up their mode of living, their habits of life, introduced disease and decay among them, and it was for this and against this they made war. Could any one expect less?"[14]

Just as they had replaced saving California for the Union with the need to defeat Indians, promoters replaced the failure of the Asian trade with hopes for a trade from the Pacific Coast and the interior. This did not work out as well as it might over the next thirty years. The initial problem with the transcontinental trade was that railroads could not compete with steamship companies. The commerce of the West Coast had a perfectly good route east; it went by sea with a short railroad passage across Panama. The route was so good that most freight continued to go that way after the first transcontinental was completed. The Union Pacific and the Central Pacific recognized that they were at the mercy of the Pacific Mail Steamship Company. With its connections by rail across Panama, the P.M.S.S. could move goods nearly as quickly as the railroads and at a much lower cost. In 1873, Jay Gould of the U.P. complained that competition from steamships, made it "outrageous that we have to carry our California business at so low rates."[15] In the late 1880s little had changed. Charles Francis Adams testified before the Pacific Railroad Commission that the Pacific Mail Steamship Company "could reduce the rate . . . until it would make the business worthless to us, and yet make something itself" on traffic to the East Coast.[16]

This was an amazing statement, one worth lingering over, for it meant that the railroads really were not necessary to move most of the freight between the East and Far West. If the Pacific Mail wished to do so, it could dominate the traffic. The question then becomes why the Pacific Mail did not do so? It didn't do so because in the 1870s and 1880s, the railroads paid the P.M.S.S. to raise their rates and limit their capacity so as to divert more traffic to the transcontinentals. The government had subsidized (I will get to the subsidies in a moment) both the railroads and the steamship company, and the two conspired to use the subsidies to raise rather than lower the cost of commerce.

Even with such subsidies, the amount of freight moving across the continent by rail was so small as to hardly figure in railroad accounts as more and more transcontinentals were finally completed. By 1885 it appeared that traffic "just sufficient" to maintain the Union Pacific and Central Pacific when they had a monopoly on the business in 1881 would have to support seven roads. The through business was by 1885 "rendered value-less by increased competition."[17] It was so subdivided among competing roads that Charles Francis Adams estimated it formed but 5 percent of the Union Pacific's entire business for 1885.[18]

In my book, *Railroaded*, I made a particular critique of the transcontinentals that some of my critics have had a hard time grasping. It goes to the particularities of railroad space during the late nineteenth-century; as railroad men understood, the space traversed by the transcontinentals was not all the same. The transcontinentals (which were not truly transcontinental) ran from the Missouri River to the Pacific Coast—or at least they aspired to do so. On both ends of this route—roughly from the Missouri River to the 98th or 100th meridian and from the Pacific Coast to the Sierra and Cascades—railroads were viable and necessary for economic development. And because they were viable and necessary for economic development, there was no need to subsidize them. They could have been, and some of the most successful were built without subsidies.

Railroads in these areas could make money by doing what well run railroads were intended to do: sell transportation at a profit. And, by and large, they did. Two sets of regional railroads: one feeding Chicago and St. Louis and one feeding San Francisco, were developed in the 1870s and 1880s. The Chicago roads were, by and large, built to meet demand and were usually solvent. The Rock Island, Chicago and Northwestern, the Burlington, and the rest restrained their desire to march off much beyond the 100th meridian and certainly restrained their desire to move across the Rockies.

The settlement of the prairies was a success, and the railroads that served settlers, while most of them received federal and state subsidies, did not require them. The best evidence that federal subsidies were unnecessary was South Dakota, which serves as a kind of natural experiment when compared to North Dakota. North Dakota had land grant railroads; South Dakota, with some minor exceptions, did not. By the 1890s, however,

South Dakota had a denser railroad network, more efficient railroads by the measure of tons carried per mile, and more farmers who had acquired land for free through the Homestead Act.

Similarly, on the West Coast into the 1890s, the real business of the Central Pacific and Southern Pacific was funneling goods into and out of San Francisco. Here, too, there was enough traffic to support regional railroads.

This leaves a vast area between roughly the 100th meridian and the Sierra and Cascades where there was not enough potential traffic to sustain a profitable railroad. This was why knowledgeable railroad men would not build transcontinentals. They preferred to build the Chicago and St. Louis roads. This left the field open to speculators and storekeepers like the Big Four. They, too, recognized the lack of traffic. "[I]t is a great country west of the Rocky Mountains in acreage," Collis P. Huntington of the Southern Pacific admitted ruefully, "and very few people on this side (the East) know how little business there is there."[19] Their goal was to make money on the traffic over the eastern and western ends of the road and channel the subsidies for the bulk of the road into their own pockets through the Credit Mobilier and Contract and Finance companies.

The subsidies were immense. The federal grant to the Union Pacific roughly equaled the square mileage of New Hampshire and New Jersey combined. The main line of the Central Pacific got slightly more than the landmass of Maryland. The Kansas Pacific had to settle for Vermont and Rhode Island. A later transcontinental, the Northern Pacific, received a total land grant that was the equivalent of converting all of New England into a strip 20 miles wide in the states and 40 miles wide in the territories, stretching from Lake Superior to Puget Sound. This did not stop it from twice going bankrupt.

In all, the land grant railroads east and west of the Mississippi received 131,230,358 acres from the United States. If all these federal land grants had been concentrated into a single state, call it Railroadiana, it would now rank third, behind Alaska and Texas, in size.[20] This largess was the main course, but there were other grants that served as a kind of dessert. The American railroads received state land grants totaling 44,224,175 acres, or an area roughly the size of Missouri, with 33 million acres alone coming from Texas, which contained no federal lands.[21] Finally, cities and towns gave the railroads valuable lands for depots, yards, and simply as inducements to create connections.[22]

In addition, the federal government gave the first transcontinental—the combination of the Union Pacific and Central Pacific called the Pacific Railway—loans of federal bonds, allowing it to build, in effect, on public credit. What the subsidies created was the possibility of making fortunes building and financing railroads, which could not sustain themselves by selling transportation.

We can argue about whether the country needed even the Pacific Railway, but I think it is hard to argue that we needed seven or more potential transcontinentals in the 1870s and 1880s.

We certainly couldn't sustain them; they went bankrupt repeatedly. To Charles Francis Adams, who assumed control of the Union Pacific, the boom in railroad building in the high plains and Rockies during the 1880s represented "a period of madness" that yielded six trunk lines across Kansas by 1893.[23] Adams seemed to scour the dictionary for synonyms for insanity, illness, and sin to portray the actions of the railroads as they overbuilt and cut rates.[24] This "mania for railroad construction" was "insanity," and it created "foolish competition."[25] He lived in a world where the "lunatics" ran the asylum.[26] The battle between the Atchison and the Southern Pacific had precipitated a "period of madness."[27] He despaired over railroad management. "[T]here is no limit to the follies they would commit."[28] The results were obvious: "we will be cutting and slashing at each other like fiends."[29] The effects would be what they had been before: "when the madness passed away the country has been strewn with the wrecks of half finished railroads."[30] And the country was.

The defense of the railroads—as they sank into bankruptcy, as insiders reaped profit, and as other investors lost money—was that while investors may have lost, the country had gained because we had the railroads. But having the railroads was not necessarily a good thing. As one English banker put it, capital had been squandered on "wild cat enterprises such as Railroads through deserts—beginning nowhere and ending nowhere."[31] Or as John Murray Forbes, a railroad man whose Burlington roads were edging west, complained that capital had been wasted on collections of rails, ties, bridges, and rolling stock "called railroads, many of them laid down in places where much of it was practically useless."[32] Charles Hassler, whose Weekly Financial Report was closely followed by investors, wrote that only through fraud had some of the lines been built, and it was "quite likely" that the country would "be better off without them."[33] Not only had the country squandered resources that could have gone elsewhere, the new roads would continue to deteriorate unless good money followed bad to maintain and improve them.³⁴

This was only the beginning of the cost. The Panic of 1873—a railroad panic prompted by the failure of the Northern Pacific Railroad—led to a depression that lasted the rest of the decade and cost workingmen their jobs and small business owners their livelihoods. There were further casualties in 1884 when western railroads failed again and, of course, still more failures in the bitter depression of the 1890s.

But there can be a counter to this, too. Certainly, if we confine our frame to the tumultuous, 1870s, 1880s, and 1890s, many railroads might appear to be a mistake, but look more broadly and their success becomes clear. The railroads may have lost money; they may have precipitated some economic hard times, but in the long run the country benefited. They enabled rapid settlement and development. A narrow financial accounting of the roads such as mine is inadequate; the social benefits of the investment that they represented—increased population, increased economic activity, the development of social institutions—has to be taken into account. This appeals to us because we find it hard, deep down, to see growth as bad. More must be better.

This is an argument of considerable weight, if true, but there are two large problems. The first is basic. By the late 1890s we do need transcontinentals, but it makes no sense to build something decades before you need it. It is no accident that the Great Northern, which best anticipated actual demand, proved the most successful of the transcontinentals. By then, costs of building had gone down and technology was much improved.

The second problem is that we can't calculate social benefits of railroads without subtracting social costs. In existing econometric analyses, social benefit calculators often have only plus signs. They do not seem to include minus signs. What if we also use a minus sign on the social benefit calculator: one that subtracts environmental damage, the harm to Indian peoples, and the collapse of industry after industry that plagued much of the West?

Let's take a brief tour of the West between 1870 and 1900. By the end of the nineteenth century, the majority of people in the western United States thought that the last twenty-five years of settlement had created a political and economic system stacked against them. And there were not only economic and political costs but also environmental. The overgrazing of the plains, the devastation of mountain forests, the decline of the bison and more all connected to the railroads. The railroads desperate search for traffic had contributed to the settlement of the interior, but this was not necessarily a good thing.

Historians sometimes say the railroads were just responding to pressure for land, but the pressure for land beyond the 98th meridian came from railroads. If demand was insatiable, why did the railroads advertise so heavily? They were not responding to a demand for settlement; they were trying to induce it, and it failed over much of the 100th meridian. Historians like water metaphors, but they use the wrong ones. Settlement was not a wave or a river but a hose, and the railroads were holding the hose.

Railroads needed traffic and would do anything to get it. They began, of course, with the destruction of the bison. The railroads hauled back the hides, and when there were no more hides, Dodge City went from being a town that shipped buffalo hides to a town that shipped cattle until the railroad pushed even cattle further west.[35]

Cattle were more likely to ride the rails into the West after the railroads expanded than walk. They certainly did not walk out since every step meant a decline in weight and a decline in value. In the winter of 1880–81, the cattle herds fell by 50 percent or more in some areas of the Great Basin as cattle froze and starved on depleted ranges. In 1884–85 the same deadly combination hit the southern plains. The combination of overgrazing, overstocking, and deadly weather moved like serial killers across the West. In 1886–87 it was the Northern Great Plains' turn. Desperate cattle raisers pushed the surviving cattle onto the market. Cattle worth $9.35 a hundred weight in 1882 brought $1 in 1887. The mechanism for moving too many cattle into most of these areas and the mechanism for moving the survivors off was the same. It was the railroads.[36]

The railroads helped promote the idea of "rain follows the plow," and they lured settlers, largely wheat farmers, out into the Great Plains. Rain follows the plow had such great appeal because in the 1880s few of the railroads' grandiose promises had been fulfilled. But rain did not follow the plow. The railroads hauled settlers into western Kansas and they hauled them out again. The railroads watched the population of western Kansas fall by nearly half between 1887 and 1897 as drought and depression struck.[37]

The growth the railroads promised was often disappointing. Even Senator John Ingalls of Kansas, the corrupt Candide of the prairies, admitted the result of expansion was that "[e]mpty railroad trains ran across deserted prairies to vacant towns."[38] California's growth was disappointingly slow.[39]

Opponents saw the railroads as sucking the state dry. Inhibiting development, Nevada had actually lost population and begun to earn its reputation as the great "rotten borough" with two US senators and pathetically few constituents. Utah remained Utah. The railroad made it more accessible, but most Americans regarded it as a polygamous embarrassment, a place inhabited by strange and exotic people. And the Central Pacific/Union Pacific were the most easily justifiable roads. The Northern Pacific, Atchison, Topeka and Santa Fe, Atlantic and Pacific, Kansas Pacific, and Texas and Pacific seemed utterly extraneous as transcontinentals when they even managed to complete their lines. Oregon and Washington relied largely on water transport and local railroads.

If all of this happened by accident, it would be one thing, but it was planned and subsidized. It yielded huge profits to insiders and great suffering to others. Economically, measured by per capita income, the condition of westerners deteriorated instead of improved.[40] Politically, westerners thought themselves plagued by monopolies and corruption, and the great model of nineteenth century monopoly was the railroad. This was, after all, what the Populists contended, and the majority of the West voted for the Populists. The states and territories along the transcontinentals were enmeshed in a system that the mass of their people thought unfair and exploitative.

In large parts of these regions, people were not only unhappy and discontented, they decided that life was not worth living in these places. In a region whose boosters emphasized opportunity, many, very often most, people failed to find it. The marks of dumb growth are all over the Great Plains and interior West to this day, in the dying towns and abandoned farms. Much area west of the 100th meridian and east of the Rockies peaked in population around 1920. It had already been the site of population retreats before that; after 1920 the decline has been relentless.[41]

* * *

My point is not that railroads should not have been built but rather that they should not have been built when they were and where they were. Delay would have worked out better for Indians, who would have had more time to adjust. It would have spared farmers who rushed into areas they could not successfully farm. It would have helped avoid the gluts of minerals, timber, and other resources that hurt the economy and the environment.

The romance of new and powerful technologies that transform the world can blind us to the full nature of the transformations. It is a lesson we are learning again today. And we are also learning today that who controls the technology is as important as the technology.

ENDNOTES

1. Henry George, "What the Railroad Will Bring Us," *The Overland Monthly* 1 (October 1868): 305.
2. Ibid.
3. Ibid.
4. Charles Francis Adams, *An Autobiography, 1835–1915, with a Memorial Address Delivered November 17, 1915 by Henry Cabot Lodge* (Boston, Houghton Mifflin, 1916), 190.
5. Central Pacific Railroad Company v. Alfred A. Cohen, *Argument of Mr. Cohen, the Defendant, in Person, before the Hon. W. P. Daingerfield, Presiding Judge without a Jury, Twelfth District Court, City and County of San Francisco* (1876), Huntington Library, 67742, p. 491.
6. Collis P. Huntington to Stanford, Oct. 25, 1871, C. Crocker, May 17, 1871, *Letters from Collis P. Huntington to Mark Hopkins, Leland Stanford, Charles E. Crocker, and E.B. Crocker,* 2: 275.
7. Collis P. Huntington to Hopkins, Jan. 3, 1873, 3: 93, Box 21, Hopkins Correspondence, in Timothy Hopkins Transportation Collection, 1826–1942, M0097, Special Collections, Stanford University.
8. Mark Hopkins to C. Huntington, Dec. 8, 1872, Collis P. Huntington Papers, 1856–1901 (Sanford, NC: Microfilming Corporation of America, 1978–79), series 1, r. 5.
9. This is widely reproduced. A copy is available at https://picturinghistory.gc.cuny.edu/john-gast-american-progress-1872/.
10. For the spike and inscription, see "Four Spikes," https://www.nps.gov/gosp/learn/historyculture/four-special-spikes.htm.
11. Paul Hutton, *Phil Sheridan and His Army* (Norman: University of Oklahoma Press, 1985), 41.
12. For policies during the Civil War, Heather Cox Richardson, *The Greatest Nation of the Earth: Republican Economic Policies during the Civil War* (Cambridge, MA: Harvard University Press, 1997), 170–72, 175, 178–80. Dodge to Scott, Jan. 12, 1874, Letterbooks, Texas Pacific Railroad, Box 160, Grenville M. Dodge Papers, MS 98, State Historical Society of Iowa, 72–73, 77; Adams to Moorfield Storey, Feb. 2, 1885, Union Pacific Railroad. Subgroup 2, Office of the President microform, Lincoln, NE: Nebraska State Historical Society, Outgoing Correspondence, v. 27, series 2, r. 23. Hereafter UPRR.
13. Quote, Adams to Moorfield Storey, Feb. 2, 1885, UPRR, Pres. Office, Outgoing Correspondence, v. 27, series 2, r. 23. For policies during the Civil War, Heather Cox Richardson, *The Greatest Nation of the Earth: Republican Economic Policies during the Civil War*

(Cambridge, MA: Harvard University Press, 1997), 170–72, 175, 178–80. See also Dodge to Scott, Jan. 12, 1874, Letterbooks, Texas Pacific Railroad, Box 160, Grenville M. Dodge Papers, MS 98, State Historical Society of Iowa, 72–73, 77.

14. Hutton, *Phil Sheridan and His Army*, 33–35; Francis Paul Prucha, *The Great Father: The United States Government and the American Indians*, 2 vols. (Lincoln: University of Nebraska Press, 1984), 1: 489–90; David H. Bain, *Empire Express: Building the First Transcontinental Railroad* (New York: Penguin, 1999), 349–52.

15. Maury Klein, *Union Pacific* (New York: Doubleday, 1987), 314.

16. Testimony of Charles Francis Adams, April 29, 1887, *Report . . . of the United States Pacific Railway Commission and Testimony Taken by the Commission*, 50th Cong., 1st Session, S. Ex. Doc. 51, 10 vols (Washington, DC: GPO, 1887–1888), 1: 110–11. CPH to Hopkins, April 19, 1875, v. 7: 131–32, Hopkins Collection; Huntington to Adams, May 18, 1886, U.P., RG 3761, Box 39, f. 5 S62 S1. Testimony of J. C. Stubbs, *Report of the Industrial Commission on Transportation . . . Testimony Taken Since May 1, 1900*, Volume IX of the Commission's Reports (Washington, DC: GPO, 1901), 763.

17. Adams to Callaway, April 22, 1886, UPRR, President's Office, Outgoing Correspondence, v. 31, ser. 2, r. 23. Adams occasionally wavered and thought through traffic would improve, Adams to Callaway, Aug. 24, 1886, UPRR, P.O., O.C., v. 32, s. 2, r. 27.

18. Adams to H. White, Dec. 3, 1885, UPRR, P.O., O.C., v. 30, s. 2, r. 26; Adams to Callaway, Oct. 10, 1885, UPRR, P.O., O.C., v. 32, s. 2, r. 28. Jules Grodinsky, *Transcontinental Strategy, 1869–93: A Study of Businessmen* (Philadelphia: University of Pennsylvania Press, 1962), 165–66. The percentage for 1886 was 8 percent. Testimony of Oliver Mink, May 24, 1887, Pacific Railway Commission, 2: 624.

19 Perkins was sobered by the business potential of the Southwest. The only business was mines. Perkins to Forbes, June 30, 1880, J. M. Forbes, In-letters, private from C. E. Perkins, 3 F 3.2–3.3. Burlington Archives, Chicago, Burlington, and Quincy Railroad Company, Newberry Library, Chicago. For Chicago, Grodinsky, *Transcontinental Strategy*, 194–95. CPH to Crocker, Dec. 8, 1881, CPH Papers, v. 29, ser. 2, r. 6.

20. The most detailed account of the railroad grants comes from *Public Aids to Transportation: Volume II, Aids to Railroads and Related Subjects* (Washington, DC: GPO, 1938), Table 13. Table 13 actually is two tables, with one table reflecting adjusted grants (i.e., with forfeited grants subtracted) for some railroads and another table reflecting unadjusted grants, where the amount lost by forfeiture or errors was not clear. Among the roads with adjusted grants, the Union Pacific received 11.4 million acres; the main line of the Central Pacific received 7.88 million acres, and the Kansas Pacific got 7.09 million acres. For those roads with unadjusted grants, the Northern Pacific got 39.4 million acres over its entire system. The entire Southern Pacific system (including the Central Pacific) received 17.9 million acres. The Atchison, Topeka and Santa Fe got 14.9 million acres. By 1933 the U.S. government had actually patented 131,230,358 acres to the railroads. The total figure and the unadjusted figures include grants later forfeited. These figures do not count nearly 4 million acres that were later voluntarily returned to settle disputes. The Canadian Pacific received 25 million acres from its government, including 6,793,014 that the Canadian Pacific surrendered in 1891 in exchange for the forgiveness of debt due the Canadian government. James B. Hedges, *The Federal Railway Land Subsidy Policy of Canada* (Cambridge, MA: Harvard University Press, 1934), 63. Also, David M. Ellis, "The Railroads and the Land Office: Administrative Policy and the Land Patent Controversy, 1864–96," *Mississippi Valley Historical Review* 46 (March 1960): 698. David M. Ellis, "The Forfeiture of Railroad Land Grants, 1867–1894," *The Mississippi Valley Historical Review* 33, no. 1 (1946): 27–60. For land grants as of 1873, see Henry V. Poor, "Congressional Land Grants for Railroads," *Manual of the Railroads of the United States 1873–74* (New York: H. V. & H. W. Poor, 1874), 696–701. For slow sales, Klein, *Union Pacific*, 514–15. By 1872 the Central Pacific claimed to have sold only $513,724 worth of land and had received $173,157. Total Sales of Lands by C.P.R.R. R. Co., including also the Cal & Oregon R.R. Co., to Jan. 1, 1872, L.B. 11: 83, Box 25, Timothy Hopkins Transportation Collection, 1826–1942, M0097, Special Collections and University Archives, Stanford University.

21. The western roads received the following amounts from the states: Nebraska, 498,742; Texas 32,990,000; Oregon, 3,200; Minnesota, 2,875,856. "Report of the Auditor of Railroad Accounts," House Ex. Doc. 1, 46th Congress, 2nd Session, 1911, Table 13, 113–15. Eventually around 35 million acres were returned, and in addition, the railroads relinquished an additional 8 million acres in 1940 in exchange for the government canceling preferential reduced rates it was entitled to receive. This created interesting geographies of land whose title was in limbo for years as railroad claims and ownership were sorted out. Leslie E. Decker, *Railroads, Lands, and Politics; The Taxation of the Railroad Land Grants, 1864–1897* (Providence RI: Brown University Press, 1964), 20–22. For additional CPR grants, see James F. Hedges, *The Federal Railway Land Subsidy Policy of Canada* (Cambridge, MA: Harvard University Press, 1934), 139.

22. *Public Aids to Transportation:* Volume II: *Aids to Railroads and Related Subjects*, 29, 111.

23. Adams to Callaway, March 18, 1886, UPRR, P.O., O.C., v. 33, ser. 2, r. 28. For Gould, L. S. Anderson to G. M. Lane, June 22, 1886, UPRR, Asst. to Pres., U.P., O.C., v. 1, L. S. Anderson, r. 1.

24. Adams to Callaway, Nov. 17, 1885, UPRR, P.O., O.C., v. 33, ser. 2, r. 26. Adams was not the only one to use such language, A. L. Williams to Adams, Dec. 15, 1886, UPRR, RG 3761, Box 44, f. 5 S62 S1.

25. Insanity, Adams to C. E. Perkins, Sept. 28, 1885, UPRR, P.O., O.C., v. 29, ser. 2, r. 25. Adams to Harris, Nov. 24, 1885, UPRR, P.O., O.C., v. 30, ser. 2, r. 26.

26. Adams to Callaway, Nov. 24, 1884, UPRR, P.O., O.C., v. 24, ser. 2, r. 21.

27. Adams to Callaway, March 18, 1886, UPRR, P.O., O.C., v. 33, ser. 2, r. 28.

28. Adams to Callaway, March 26, 1885, UPRR, P.O., O.C., v. 33, ser. 2, r. 28.

29. Adams to Perkins, Sept. 19, 1885, UPRR, P.O., O.C., v. 29, ser. 2, r. 25.

30. Adams to Hon. P. B. Plumb, Nov. 9, 1885, UPRR, P.O., O.C., v. 30, ser 2, r 26.

31. *Standard*, Oct. 24, 1874, Newspaper Cuttings Files of the Council of Foreign Bondholders in the Guildhall Library, London, 1874–93, reel 219. *National Car Builder* quoted in *Railway Age* 1 (Oct. 19, 1876): 343; "Capital and Railroad Extension," *Bankers' Magazine and Statistical Register* 10 (Oct. 1876): 279. Lees & Waller to Mills, Ralston, and Bell, Dec. 7, 1872, Lees & Waller to Bell, Dec. 9, 1872, box 3, 5, W. C. Ralston Papers, MO 217, Special Collections, Stanford University.

32. Quoted in Gerald Berk, *Alternative Tracks: The Constitution of American Industrial Order, 1865–1917* (Baltimore: The Johns Hopkins University Press, 1994), 38.

33. "The Truth Needed about Railroads," *Railway Age* 1 (Oct. 19, 1876): 372. "American Railroad Credit," *Railway Age* 3 (Jan. 10, 1878): 20.

34. "Losses in Railway Securities," *The Railway Age*, (March 22, 1877): 802; *Public Aids to Transportation:* Volume II: *Aids to Railroads and Related Subjects* (Washington, DC: GPO, 1938), 18–19.

35. Drew Isenberg, *The Destruction of the Bison* (New York: Cambridge University Press, 2000), 157–60.

36. Richard White, "Animals and Enterprise," in Clyde Milner, Carol A. O'Connor, and Martha Sandweiss, eds., *The Oxford History of the American West* (New York: Oxford University Press, 1994), 266.

37. For continued building, Adams to Callaway, May 15, 1886, U.P., P.O., O.C., v. 38, ser. 2, r. 33. Lease of Central Branch, Adams to Perkins, Oct. 2, 1885, U.P., P.O., O.C., v. 29, ser. 2, r. 25. For Shelby, "Freight Department (1885), P. P. Shelby in Freight and Passenger Earnings, 1885," UPRR, MS 3761, unnumbered box, p. 131. Scott G. McNall, *The Road to Rebellion: Class Formation and Kansas Populism, 1865–1900* (Chicago: University of Chicago Press, 1988), 79. Also, O. Gene Clayton, *Kansas Populism: Ideas and Men* (Lawrence: University Press of Kansas, 1969), 29–30. For rain follows the plow, David M. Emmons, *Garden in the Grasslands: Boomer Literature of the Central Great Plains* (Lincoln: University of Nebraska Press, 1971).

38. John James Ingalls, *A Collection of the Writings of John James Ingalls: Essays, Addresses, and Orations* (Kansas City, MO: Hudson-Kimberly Publishing Co., 1902), 478.

39. Despite the Civil War, California grew by 47 percent between 1860 and 1870 without the railroad. It grew by 54 percent between 1870 and 1880 with the railroad, reaching 864,694 people. It had grown more slowly and was smaller than Kansas. Calculated from Historical Census Browser, University of Virginia Library, http://fisher.lib.virginia.edu/collections/stats/histcensus/. Richard Orsi, *Sunset Limited: The Southern Pacific Railroad and the Development of the American West, 1850–1930* (Berkeley: University of California Press, 2007), 130, 193–204, 323–29.

40. See "Per Capita Income in the United States, 1880–1900," Shaping the West, Spatial History Project, Stanford University, https://web.stanford.edu/group/spatialhistory/cgi-bin/site/viz.php?id=259&project_id=0.

41. McNall, *Road to Rebellion*, 79–80.